Exactly As I Am

Rae White is a non-binary transgender writer, author, educator and zine maker. Their poetry collection *Milk Teeth* (UQP, 2018) won the 2017 Arts Queensland Thomas Shapcott Poetry Prize, was shortlisted for the 2019 Victorian Premier's Literary Awards and commended in the 2018 Anne Elder Award. Rae's poem 'The last tourist' won Highest Queensland Entry in the 2020 Arts Queensland Val Vallis Award. Their poem 'what even r u?' placed second in the 2017 *Overland* Judith Wright Poetry Prize. Rae's poetry has been published in *Australian Poetry Journal*, *Cordite Poetry Review*, *Meanjin*, *Overland*, *Rabbit* and other publications. Rae is the editor of *#EnbyLife* (enbylife.net), a journal for non-binary and gender diverse creatives. They are the Events and Marketing Manager at Queensland Poetry.

raewhite.net

Also by Rae White

Milk Teeth

Rae **White**

Exactly As I Am

For Jesse

First published 2022 by University of Queensland Press
PO Box 6042, St Lucia, Queensland 4067 Australia
Reprinted 2023

University of Queensland Press (UQP) acknowledges the Traditional Owners and
their custodianship of the lands on which UQP operates. We pay our respects to their
Ancestors and their descendants, who continue cultural and spiritual connections to
Country. We recognise their valuable contributions to Australian and global society.

uqp.com.au
reception@uqp.com.au

Cover design by Sandy Cull, www.sandycull.com
Author photograph by Chloë Callistemon
Typeset in 11.5/14 pt Bembo Std by Post Pre-press Group, Brisbane
Printed in Australia by McPherson's Printing Group

 **Queensland Government** University of Queensland Press is supported by the
Queensland Government through Arts Queensland.

  University of Queensland Press is assisted by
the Australian Government through the
Australia Council, its arts funding and
advisory body.

A catalogue record for this book is available from the National Library of Australia.

ISBN 978 0 7022 6549 5 (pbk)
ISBN 978 0 7022 6670 6 (epdf)
ISBN 978 0 7022 6764 2 (epub)
ISBN 978 0 7022 6765 9 (kindle)

Content warning: poems in this book include references to transphobia, queerphobia,
misgendering, deadnaming, death, surgery and hospitals, body horror, allusions to self
harm, and sexual harassment.

University of Queensland Press uses papers that are natural, renewable and recyclable
products made from wood grown in well-managed forests and other controlled sources.
The logging and manufacturing processes conform to the environmental regulations of
the country of origin.

MIX
Paper | Supporting
responsible forestry
FSC® C001695

Contents

Exclaim

Exhale

Exalt

Exclude

Lifelike
After Lisa Adams's Inquisition *(oil on canvas, 2016)*

      Disinfect and find blood-lit lichen
staining an eyelid. Incision reveals incisors
blooming with teratoma independence in left
cheek pocket. We scoop and discard, slice
to make space
      to sterilise. Feathers droop
soaked and blush-heavy in a slick
steel basin.   *How could anyone*
    live like this?   I wince when a tooth, scalpel-
sharp, punctures my glove. The next day, I bleed
blue, and the next, my fingertip swells
      erythristic plumage.

gut punch

outstretched and flat-packed, we stack tabular and rebuild
you, under hot gaze of sickly bright
lights. wafer paper is
abandoned (no instructions
worthy   of this one). we apprentice

in transmutation: the upright habits of neck
veins and table legs, the whorl patterns of red
guts and timber. we whisper devotions over jangling
allen keys, above static shuffle of nurses'
footsteps.   shoes come last –

plastic baby-small protectors snapped
into place, as if that's enough to stone-
wall   from this one.

Vital signs

Monitor me, guardedly: pulse
points   temperature   temperament   fast
heart   heart-hardened. My gender: elevated
rhythmic   medically
unsound.

Hussshhh

I walk into the women's
toilets and the unravelling de-
gendering of it makes my head
tilt below my collarbone. Someone
clears their throat. 'But I thought you were enby?'
Yes
and scientists have discovered The Radical
Genderqueer pees only in spaces
not dedicated to them, as a sign of respect
for the binary. Toilet cistern's hiss
sounds like the act
of silencing: ssshhh
you're more effective
when you're quiet.
Hussshhh, speak
under not over
the toilet, crawl right in
between brush and bowl. Whispers
between stalls: *ssshhh eee she*
is less talkative
these days; I think their species
is learning.

magic 8-ball

⑧

carved-out globe ⑧ tic-tac rattle ⑧ plastic-on-
plastic ⑧ click-clack twist ⑧ blue
food-colour slosh ⑧ 'without a doubt'
I will be misgendered
for the rest
of my life ⑧
that when it comes to
poetry ⑧ 'outlook is good'
but as for pronouns ⑧ 'don't
count on it'
⑧
⑧

Transactions

Forms, questions, card re-
issues, questions ...
I legally change my name.
         On rainy days, my transport card
stops working. All the trains on all lines
stop working. My Medicare card perfectly
snaps in half. My passport
              blackens at the edges and
                       disintegrates.

When my new bank card arrives
it's then I question:
         am I being phased out
              of society?

TRANS NOT APPROVED

Sorry that didn't work. Is there
         money left
                  on the card?

TRANS NOT APPROVED

Do you want to try another card, sir?
I mean, ma'am?
         I mean?
              Uh ... ?

TRANS NOT ACCEPTED

You might need to swipe or insert.

It's about the action, you see,
the way you hold
your card. We just know, when we look
at you and we don't approve
of your card and your card is an extension
       of you and your worth.
             Do you see?

My kink is late capitalism, baby

$

Can I be your driven
go-getter? Your casual boi Thursday?
I have extensive experience and a good
degree hanging translucently loose off my frame.
Can you see my nipples? I wanna sit on your lap, baby,
while you drill me about attention to detail and working
autonomously. I get so hot just thinking of your waxing moon-
smooth chest and bulging   financial capital. And I know we
both get hard ruminating the gap between my wage and your
fortune. God, does your back hurt   or is it just me? Baby, just
tell me I'm fucked already, that I'm nothing   but the fruit
without the pit, the hard work without the reward. Tell me
my low market value as you empty loose change onto
my tits. I could come   but I don't. Are you
dizzy too? You shift on the bed and coins
tremble   from   bedazzled
flesh   to   floor.

$

Check in
With respect to the Eagles

QR code flickers fuzzy on phone screen
as you scan. Pooling of tight masked breaths.
Type quick for green-tick proof, then sanitise
up to your elbows. Don't forget to check out.

There's nothing quite so sterile as standing
1.5 metres from plant life – 'If you touch, you buy.'
Shelves are picked over, fertiliser and food
sold out. Potted Pothos calls to you

with gaunt limbs outstretched.
You purchase an unassuming Zanzibar
instead. Better be safe than sorry.
Flash your card at self-serve and notice

you're in the negative. You reach doorway
but bump backwards, like fleeting bird
against window glass. The exit's aura
fizzes and flexes. You forgot to check out.

With new plant nestled against hip, stretch out
your left hand for phone but feel only the sweat
of your own skin.

It's gone. It's giggling in the green-leaf clasp
of the Pothos, battery almost dead.

Air-con breeze that sounds almost like breathing rustles against your earlobes. Leaves waver and twist like beckoning, like stalking, like hunting.

You can't ever leave.

Do more, do better

1.

Trans Shield changes the way you see
the world, even if the world
          sees you differently.
Until society catches
up, there's an app
          for that!

Just want people to respect
your identity? Pissed at being
politely misgendered when you
          just want to buy your fucking
          groceries? Want Gran
to use he/him but she's not quite
getting it and she might kick
          the bucket soon
          and the whole situation is bloody
          upsetting?

Simply plug your name/s,
          pronoun set/s and
          preferred terms (e.g. guy,
          girl, ma'am, dude,
          person)
into Trans Shield and you're good
          to go!

Every time the wrong
        crap is used in relation
to you, you won't even hear that
        shit. Our app syncs with your
BrainChip and uses the latest
AR breakthroughs
to overlay onto the
person who wilfully
        fucked up
        so you won't even notice
        they did. (Multiple options
are available, including realistic
        glazes of hands
and sign language, or a voice
        and mouth.)

Once you have this
app, every instance of
        'oi tr★nny sl★t!'
        hurled at you
        on the street
will be masked
by the phrase
of your choice, including: 'trans rights
        are human rights!' or 'TERFs suck
        hey?!'

For an additional
in-app fee you can replace
slurs from cars with a golden
        retriever, barking joyously, their head thrust

unceremoniously out the window, feeling
the breeze ruffle
        their silky ears.

2.

Additional features
        of Trans Shield include
                the ability to:

- put the app in Sleep
  Mode, so you can discover
  which of your uncles at family
  dinner is misgendering you and
  address the issue head-on
  by telling him
  to get fucked.
- use multiple profiles and switch
  between them on a frequent or in-
  frequent basis. Perfect for anyone
  who's bigender or genderfluid.
- edit any of your details
  at any time because
  who says we can't explore
  who we are!

3.

Latest Trans Shield update:
Unfortunately we are still unable
to address user concerns regarding
violence against
transgender and gender diverse
people,
        especially
        violence against and the
        murder of
        transgender women of colour.

Nor can we address the broader
systemic issues relating to
        the way society views
        and treats us
within the current scope
of this app. We are truly
        sorry.

4.

Our sister app
Be Fucking Nicer,
which was marketed
at cisgender people, allowed the user
to store people's pronouns and
identities for future
social interactions, and included
        gamified education
        tools (such as Ally
        Credit Cookies).

We are sad to announce
this app was taken
down from the store for breaking
the terms of service. The terms
stated that: in this
day and age of 'full
        equality' we are not allowed to unduly
influence the minds and decisions
of cisgender people
in this way. Again, we are truly
        sorry. We wish we could
        do more, do better.

The Truest Crime

Podcast tells you to pincer my larynx
in one hand, your penis gently
flaccid in the other. Send a stream
off the balcony, staining the scorched
summer roadside. I hear: the hiss
below and the intimate wheeze
of my lungs. You hear: Episode 2
which recommends burial, concrete
sarcophagus coating my skin, pressing
on my organs. Will the loud
shaft of a drill ever find me? Punch straight
down my mouth then up up up to crack apart
my seashell skull? Podcast tells you to pause
and pray over me. Rough knees atop my
pelvis as you crouch and listen to breezes
breathe life into bulldozers and cranes
circling you in worship.

Bloody

It's almost midnight
again. I'm on tiptoe, unbalanced
tiles judging chapped
soles. I'm picking
pimples in the mirror
with glee by candlelight. My nose
bruised plum, bloodied pink. I sigh
my name, watch my lip's cold sore
quiver. I repeat, this time louder
each vowel tasted and earned.
A third time and my grainy
lips stretch and tingle, split
kiss-crag and I'm bleeding
into my own mouth. The mirror's
current ripples, swelling in response to
worthy   suffering
                and fatigue.

And there they are:

        a future self-spectre
                spellbound   flickering
                clear-skinned   sleep-full
                smiling

I'm transfixed, transported
to prospects and what-ifs, bargaining
with myself, briskly neglecting
the fateful crescendo:

transgender

Tentative, I kiss the mirror
and bloody up my own mouth's
evolution. It's almost
midnight again.

Customer Feedback Survey

1. On the following scale how would you rate his/her commitment to his/her role?
   1 2 3 4 5 6 7 8 9 10
2. Would you say his/her enthusiasm is sky-diving high or does he/she not really dedicate his/her singular life to this job and your consumption of his/her identity / appearance / existence?
   1 2 3 4 5 6 7 8 9 10
3. Please note: He/she has to give his/her ALL and everyone has to see how much he/she is trying to look like us, to walk and talk like cis, to reach ultimate trans KPIs, to be the best most palatable person possible.
4. Because normalisation / assimilation / cis-ification into society is his/her goal
5. isn't it?
   ☑ ☒
6. If he/she doesn't commit, doesn't dedicate his/her life to This Perfection, then what is the point / end result / intention?
   1. What do they want?
      Answer: _____
   2. What are they for?
      Answer: _____

Side effects

of this medication may/may not include:

- nausea or vomiting or diarrhoea
  or none
  or all of these
- hair loss or hair growth anywhere on
  (or in)
  the body
- fluid retention or increased
  urination
- furious acne or lush
  clear skin
- breast growth or reduction
  or nipple
  discolouration or increased
  sensitivity or
  none of these (or
  all of these
  in painful rotation)
- depression or happiness or anxiety
  or an obnoxious
  enthusiasm for life
  or the exact opposite
- increased or decreased or fairly mediocre
  sex drive
- sudden genital arousal or numbness
  or size fluctuations, such as growth
  or shrinkage
- undesirable male or female
  characteristics, employing

arbitrary categorisation
and socialised
transphobia
- or none
  or all
  or some
  of the above

: paint me over

i suspect the poised surface
of me is a post-photo nightmare
to you. i watch you watch me
bend over: the creak and heat
of my back   unrelenting.

could you commodify this?   : the pink
of me as I slink and relax, objectified
in the shallows: cold leaves palming
the back of my neck. tell me : am I trope
or trouble to you? is my portraiture
distraction or abstraction? finding it hard
to decide between only two readings?
same   babe   same.

some days i feel like the only way
to transcend
is to ask you to   : oil me up;
spittle me with colourful
flecks; dismantle and curve my de-
gendered bones: god, just 3D print me
new ones crafted from second-hand
canvases; just peel and paint me over
already. so both our biases are blemish-
cleansed   yes   yes:

I think I'm finally   ready.

Exist

if there's nothing out there,
                           why am I searching?

translucent pink
aerial roots prowling   pushing
                               into steam-thick air.

sucking moisture
from breezes to thicken
skin, devouring   funnelling
                               sunlight for strength.

limbs wrinkled, leaves
sunken, sockets of dry   dirt
                               blanketing terrain.

house-bound in the cursed rental

unhinged: our world
when the screen door is installed
upside down. there are no longer forks
only knives. bamboo transforms to bonsai, emulating
our air-tight claustrophobia. our cat walks   diagonally up
walls, only eats bulb-scalded   moths that flounce at twiggy
lamps. our hair the feeble limbs of lavender plants   we recently killed.

Hot, cold

I leave clothes at every house
I'm welcomed in to. Shed undershirt in shadowed
wash basket, swap out sock couples from drawers, plant
unsuspecting undies under yours
in the thin light. Bury everything warmly
in this garden soil but with a bright
new leaf jutting out so you can
      find me again.

I drop clothes like talismans because you never know
when you might need a cardie or a scarf. Isn't it cold
in here? I say, subtly dropping mittens
into medicine cabinet. Don't you
      feel freezing?

You ask, will there be a next time? Of course
because you already own pieces
of me. I'm not sorry to say I climbed in
through the window last night to stitch
stockings into your carpet, to splice a new necklace
with your heirloom bracelet. Did you notice
how I dropped one slipper down the side
of the stairwell? The other lifeless and alone
      at the last step.

home watchful and dust
home dustful and blanch
float up and up and sight-
switch to fright
something moves and up
and off to float up
something dreaming of others
something dreaming of dust
moves again and out
moves out up off
switch-blink in the scrub
vex-self in the splice-shift
home switch-blink and up
and flicker and off
fright floating in dream-self
flight flicker switch-off
home watchful and dust
home dustful and blanch
float up and up and sight-
switch to fright
something moves and up
and off to float up
something dreaming of others
something dreaming of dust
moves again and out
moves out up off

switch-blink in the scrub
vex-self in the splice-shift
home switch-blink and up
and flicker and off
fright floating in dream-self
flight flicker switch-off
home watchful and dust
home dustful and blanch
float up and up and sight-
switch to fright
something moves and up

What have you done?

I'm windowsill watchful as they scuttle
to pack suitcases, boxes, green bags, duffels.
All spilling over warmly like waterfalls.
We could do with the rain. Sky hazes red
with thick-brimmed clouds as their breathing
hardens and hastens, running from car to door
and back again. Forearm lengths of forehead sweat
wiped and flicked to floor. Sharpened sunlight
folds through my window and bathes my leaves
orange. What is leaving when you're simply left
behind? Because just like that, no more bags.

> *We forgot the plant!* someone shouts
> over sirens. Door ajar for a second's hesit-
> ation before: *Leave it, just leave it!*
> *It'll fend for itself* ...

Don't feed

Don't feed
Don't feed

Turns out maggies like Schmackos.
If their black-white feathers
look bedraggled and spent

chances are they're old and without
teeth, so halve flat egg-shaped treat
and throw it directly

in open beak. Like a bard
they'll thank you with
repetitive song.

Turns out one maggie
brings many. Soon you'll have
a baker's dozen

basking on the bitumen
at your feet. Don't be alarmed
when the 13th is a crow.

I think that's lucky
perhaps. Anything is lucky
in years like this – if birds

if birds
if birds
if birds

are alive and you're outside
count yourself. Count your teeth
behind your mask. And ask yourself

how many teeth is the right
amount? How many
is too many?

Turns out birds don't have teeth
but their beaks and swoops
are just as sharp.

Fling all the Schmackos
in their direction as diversion
and run. Government guidelines state

masks must be worn during exercise
and hasty escapes. You don't know
which this is but you do know

sweat crawls against your
spine and your muggy breath
wheezes up your nose.

Turns out you should've read
the new sign. Things have
changed round here.

Turns out beaks aren't
just for swallowing
Schmackos or seed

skin
or sinew

scapula
or scalp.

Turns out no matter your
fitness or kindness
you can't outrun

the birds
the birds
the birds

as climate change descends,
i wait to be immortalised

museum is soft
without the scurry.

thick air wraps me
in scarves. behind this glass

i'm so catastrophically
tired. if i stay displayed

for long enough, will i too be
catalogued, preserved?

objectify and name me,
please, register me

as unique and let me sleep here
                              in peace.

a half-eaten succulent
addresses the possum

i was peace
-fully full & full
of content. sun
-brushed & plump
with water & swollen
memories. you ate

my new leaf, my lush
new branch, pushed
& cracked
my neck. i'm sorry
i'm invasive.
i'm sorry you're so
very hungry. i hope

i tasted perhaps
like a dream.

made your bed

we're deeped and plenty
in this ocean. buoyed
to feast on flotsam
snow, to scavenge softly
for carcass. biolumine-
scent, we wait for you.
flashlit, we listen
for eyeshine.

Visitors

Why do you talk
about the possums that way?

Only one visible: coat plump and brown-plum.
A wiry nest cuddled under outdoor plant stand
sphered in: curved branches, tethered twine, old man's
beard (crumpled), clustered fairy lights (clutched
and dragged) from the garden.

Because I don't know their gender, I say.
Or there could be two of them.

I watch your furry breath-belly swell and
exhale. We all have to breathe. And maybe
you have nowhere else to go.

A snickering response: *Well, aren't you just*
a goddamn warrior!

Jumbled twigs shuffle and shutter
pops: your shiny black eye
watching us. We've been too loud.

the burning & the _____

an iron is either hot or
cold water in a vase with
wildflowers *burn at your*
touch the plate to melt your
palms *beached & aflame as the planet*
protests the chanting extremes

my extremities blistering
purple & _____

_____ *while the iron is partially*
warm my hands between your
thighs *brushing flowers & knees*
sunken beside the grave

toes nestled in artificial
sand & _____

seagulls choke on the iron
cord noosing our ankle
bones *of chicken sucked*
dry like _____ in winter

morning forgets to awaken

                        n

my knife, your torchlight   n
we ____ past the burning
& the _____ toward
_____, wondering

when hibernation will begin   n
                              n   n
                                          n   n
                                                              n

{we three are witness

to the golden hour. you are clean}cloaked and the tiles
are golden: splatter}bright in the bathroom lights,
echo}reflective like freshly laid snow
in gold{dawn headlights. stray flecks of flaxen
bleach your leg hair
golden. we missed a spot. would you
have missed us? you quaver
from blood{loss as my arm trembles
from haematic panning. you could make
four gold angels
in all   this snow}

Somewhat safe

At the airport, on different sides
of the country, we're both
ushered. *Sir-ma'am, just a random
test for explosives.*
I message you: *It happened again.*
Same, you type. *Do you think it was
the tattoos? It was probably
the skirt.*

In different stores in different states
buying the same cheap blue
hair dye, you get your bags
checked. *Ma'am-sir, just a random
check, part of our store policy.*
You message me: *You too?*
Nah, I type. *Got me some cis-passing
white privilege, baby.*

On quiet streets, we're walking
home. Wind tickles the river, ripples
cool air down my neck, reminds me
of rotating fans hemmed with ice trays
in summer. In this moment
I'm happy, somewhat safe.

You message me: *Was just yelled at
on the street. Again. Thought
they were gonna stop,*

get out of the car. Can I
call you?

My heart
shucked and floundering
on the footpath. A car creeps
down the unlit side street
with headlights howling.

You can always call me.

Gender marker

You fax the emailed printed
scanned copy
of the copy
of the copy
of the govt form to the sun-cracked machine
on the beach. The waves lap
it up coz they love
repetition. Tiny hermit crabs tinker
across the square plastic edges
tickling the machine with their
claws. It laughs, grey skin splitting in fissures
choking out faxes with guffaws. Paper's strewn
akimbo on the beach where
X marks the spot
      X marks the
          X marks
            X

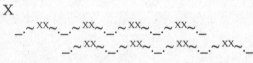

In the end, it's all in the ocean
Xs cruising waves like they own
the joint. And maybe they do
in the end. In the end,

even the crabs
slide out with the tide.

were

i take a bus   to your funeral
goes right past Pashen Street
right past that towering tree
where we used to
well
y'know

and it's about 32   even in air-con
bus clattering
as cheese platter sweats
to my thighs   bricks and biscuits
yellow and white
under misted cling film

i'm too nervous to read   but
(to be unfair)   i wasn't even asked
i'm important enough
for catering
cheapo cheese from Aldi
on Mum's best Kmart platter
but not important enough
for the usual
suit tie
speech

i promised you i'd wear   earplugs
i have 'em in my pocket   ready to go
my quiet resistance   clear bulbs
discreet and tucked   so i can't hear

your dead name   can't hear you be
      degendered   unbuilt

all i'll hear
is shell echoes
sea whispers
remembering you
exactly
as you were

#NatureIsHealing

Ibis are looking cleaner, snowier
when I go on my designated walks.
Less plump, more gloss (like they've bathed

in the very best hair conditioner).
I don't remember the last time
I showered. But I smell like exercise

and exercise is acceptable and jigsaws
are legal and groceries are constitutional.
If I get my groceries delivered, who else

do I put at risk? I join a mutual aid group,
cook food in bulk in my home, ladle serves
into name-labelled containers

and it smells like the preface to a potluck
in the park. (Bring a plate, bring a friend.)
I haven't hugged my friends

in months. I've attended too many
Zoom funerals. (Don't forget, turn video off
when you cry.) I want that damp smell

of early morning air, overturned soil,
brine of tears. I haven't been misgendered
in months. The jolt of a pause before

a missing pronoun gasps me back
to the present like an echo.
I think I've been dis-

-associating. I think the glare around me
is too bright, as the person
with the dog tells us we're both

'good girls'. (I think I'm very tired.)
I just want that fabric softener smell
of home. I just want to go home.

Discussing polyamory in the workplace:

I don't.

Forgive me, partners, for I have fucked
up. I said *her* and omitted you and you
and you and you and   all of you.

Is this feeling the sweaty pool-dive terror
of lying or is this more like   survival?

But it's a new decade!   *We got the yes vote!*
We're here and queer and we'll never be silenced
again but how do we calibrate
silence if my yeses

                                                  are many?

Because in the concrete heat of this warehouse lunchroom
my creative licence is luminous: you're my blue- and brown-

eyed girlfriend who does yoga and makes RPGs and works

in IT in economics in retail in nursing in publishing

in – GOD! You contain multitudes! You're a mega-girlfriend multi-

talented enigma. You're everything this enby could want in a wife

but what if one   could never be enough?

A single partner does not

this polycule make.

Forgive me, colleagues, for I am not precisely

who you think I am. Discussing polyamory

in the workplace?

            I don't.

    But maybe in this next decade   I will.

now > winter

i dissolve sideways > snow-washed pine needles grip to gap flesh < hibernation lips wintered
to breathe back a > fogged hush in your mouth < kissing you was always the plan > kissing
you has always been resistance : an act of wet-teethed performance art < stepping stones
through queer-soaked history : please hold me > down hold me close as the world collapses
concave > breathe boldly and kiss me > fill my lungs with our bones :

the island rule(r)
For Ōkunoshima (Rabbit Island)

dusty trails stretch
      forward   and   forward and
no amount of squinting
~~with hand-shading eyes~~
can determine its length.

sun spotlights: a slumping fort
      squatting stale ~~and crumpled~~
in the distance. you sit exhausted
and knobble-boned
on flat rock, tailbone twinging.

and like mirage they appear
      as ~~hasty~~ miracle
      in your line of sight: from ravine
of rustle-foliage a kangaroo muzzle and capybara-
body twitch ~~quizzically~~
jacked hindquarters
nudging forward with
      step   not   hop.

the rabbit king   you awe-whisper
eliciting a snarl-like grunt.

      ((~~if you get on your knees~~
      ~~in the dirt will you be forgiven?~~))

I'm sorry   you say
        holding up palm
~~dewy with sweat~~   *I didn't know*
anything else   *was here.*

head cocked like loyal dog
with small ears flexed.

anyone, I meant
        ((anyone))

to rest

settled in boat of milk carton
halved, fingertips brushing
feathers from eyelids. I'm sorry

for all this ceremony. sister sighs
behind me, texting. I drown
out her deadleaf footshuffle

as I bear you to river's edge,
your body vibrant against
the hurried creek. *I'm sorry I never*

taught you to talk, I whisper
before pushing you
out and off to bathe

and race and finally
to rest.

The last tourist

For the birds at Tangalooma, Moorgumpin (Moreton Island)

White-bellied sea-eagle

it was a sight to sea me, bird of pray nip cormorant
neck n yank clean off, blood flushing beige
sand red, her wedding dress   now russet as screams
swoosh me to abandon my picnic   but no, thank u
i'll keep ripping n rummaging 'til every organ
morsel is skinned   n gorged

Bush stone-curlew

My party trick? I stay up all day and only sleep
when the very last tourist does. But there's always one
awake, torso tipping, guts splashed up
in the garden like upended beer bottle.
I've only had alcohol once, funnelled with pincer beak
as beetle chaser. Tasted like seawater
gone vinegar. I live in this 90s paradise with Michael
Jackson tunes swelling near signs flashing
WordArt fonts. My knees ache swollen and I still feel
hungover. I'm a life jacket
        time loop, a nocturnal
            error. I'm one scream away
                from erratic rebirth.

Whistling kite

Cheeee chk chk   chk chk   cheeee! Cheeee
chk chk   chk chk   cheeee!

White-faced heron

Harry's wedding was a tragic sight: two lanky grey birds
preening and feather fluffing 'I dos' – then whiptail flash
and swoop   of white
and she   was gone, tucked up
     limp   in grappler claws.

Now bride haunts shoppers' finger-smudged window
as groom's ghost-grey reflection. He paces
     and fusses,   paces
         and waits.   She should
         be back soon.

Welcome swallow

softly born & tourist-raised in boneyard
     museum of eggshell & nest …… a living artifact
sailing on air-con winds, asking …… *Can I land*
     on your shoulder? …… I weigh almost
nothing …… Can I land
     on your shoulder? …… Can I land ……

Pelican

I'm countershaded like cormorant: burnt
on top, bleached under belly, like a flipped
Top Deck chocolate, like bleeding mud
inking snow. You fling silver fish spiny-head first
and I swallow it whole.

      I enveloped a Chihuahua once: joyous jaw-full of dog
            until companion yanked leash like flossing.
      I always want what I shouldn't have. Like fish-filled bucket
            all to myself. Like hand, plastic, hook.

Exclaim

life outside the pouch

the weather is 33, feels like a slow grill 29: an analogy
for my age, when I see the 5 boomers glowing
on the sprawling acreage. not 6, like the prophecy said,
but 5: necks wire|taut and tails muscle|thick.

only 2 are white, sun|bleached with manicured
grey eyebrows. the other 3 are tanned, golden|sinew
coats glinting and syrupy like hot oil.

reminds me I crave the grease|tan
of a dagwood dog, want to leisurely lick
the tomato sauce trickling down my forearm.
but it's an august once|a|year delicacy
like woolies avocados at 2|for|5 bucks.
a treat. unlike the 3 casual jobs I stack
and layer like wizened sweaters
because I can't get warm, can't afford
a doona or that deep|fried dog, can't
afford to be standing here: a luxury

to watch as the 5 of them grumble and chomp
5cm clipped store|bought lawn
with health|funded teeth and cancer|free jaws
because what kind of roo needs a ciggie
just to get through the day? speaking of

did you know the 2 sides of their lower jaws
aren't joined? hence their bites are massive
yawns and their teeth grind down, push

forward like white entitlement in a restaurant
line, before falling out and being replaced.

ringtail, in memoriam

5 ▼

en route to work, i see you: pelt shadowed & swollen
with rain, your eyes quarter-closed. next day
you sleep in shrubbery, footpath streaked
with ants fidgeting in your
blood/guts/piss.

4 ▼

soon you're unrecognisable, swamped
with beetles/crows/flies: their glistening work
takes weeks, they nibble & shift against
flesh, tickle at cooking sun-soaked
muscle.

3 ▼

in the office, my boss
laments the declining state
of the world: the neediness of 'transes'
in workplaces (example: bathrooms
always bathrooms, the demands of our
inconclusive genitals). i wonder about you
only halfway down the road & gleaming
with decay. i wonder what your life was like
on wires, tightrope-skittering above men
like him.

2 ▼
next day my corporate-polished shoes sweat
& slip. i notice we both look dishevelled:
my morning selfie reeks of pimples/slumped
shoulders/alcohol. you are ground-sunk
hairs fanning back & sleeping
into leaf litter, the curves
of your bones exposed
sunlit & glowing.

1 ▼
after a workday where he tries to touch
my inner thigh ('accidental' slip, searching)
i watch the local cat (ghost-like/light-
reflective/crease-faced) rolling
next to you: shifting corpse-spine
against cat-spine, unaware she's tumbling
in your grave.

0 △
it's a total of six months (the honeymoon
period) before you're looking good
as new. i slowly curl curved
tail (bleached/white/intact) from the over-
grown grass, domino it flat into my chipped
takeaway container. i resign.

poach   breach

mouth plum   hushed
heart juiced   beached
and bruised   blossoms
wetly prone   we resist
ripen   redly
gasp   golden

pre-passive
After James Gleeson's Primavera (oil on canvas, 1953)

two washed lemon-gold with trampling   tawny-toes ; coaxing fingertips
across salt-lips of moon-licked   mouths ; feathery pits   smooth-greased
in awe ; docile petals   like hair pinch-plucked ; pincers   chatter

a swollen omen ;;

but you're busy pushing   tongue-muscle against the pomegranate
of my eye ; we've lived alongside each other   so long ; only now
you wish to see   what I'm made of ;;   but you should know
my mollusc-tickled biceps   are more bite   than flex ;

so please , pumice

my glisten-cheeks with your palm ; unfold   lichen-limbs to stretch-strain
to inspect   to gawp   to ignore   the sharp wink of warning ;;

I've got something to say

Will I always be   scowling, cowering
up tops of trees under   stars, slumping
my shoulders? Will I always be media-
frenzied and flung under palatable rainbow
buses? Will I always be   a warning   a cautionary tale
to you? i.e. keep the   kids away from
that one: a 'genderqueer' (sic) costs
an arm and a leg and   hormones
to upkeep. Don't buy it, don't engage, let sleeping dogs
lie to me like I'm someone   you don't   want to hurt.

 When everything else in your life is sturdy
 statements, why am I the   question?
 Why do I ask, can you   love me (as I am)?
 Rather, that you should   (be happy) to love me
 in sickness and amidst my   unhealthy eating
 habits. Thus I have (timidly) written: please
 plead with me your case of   shame at my
 buffet of sins because could I not be   your blessing
     cloaked as that baby   you once assigned   and held?

taste ~ silver ~

heart attacks like ~~ gravestones
on ECG^^^jitter~box
chest scars pressed together
taste tick of each beat ...

on ECG jitter~box ^^^
echoes like new velvet
taste tick of each ... beat
sweat-lashed \\ cracked lips

echoes ...... like new velvet
I hear ridges of each line ____
sweat-lashed cracked \ lips \
our scars {moonstoned}silver

I hear ridges }} of each line
\pressed together\ like velvet
our scars moonstoned~~silver
our scars only ours ...~~~

wanna cyber??? ;)))

the walls r crisp perfect
squares & everything is grey.
my screen name has numbers
in place of words. i'm attracted
2 the way u type in ALL CAPS.
u ask ONE haunting shouting
question – A/S/L? as if that's all
a person can b :///
i'm 33 but my creaking
shoulder feelz like 40.
i'm 16 again pretending
2 b 18. i'm 18 again pretending
2 b less tired. i'm F again pretending
2 b M pretending 2 b F ... but what if this isn't
pretend anymore?
what if play became life
outside this grey box?
coz sex is just as much a construct
as gender & we're both
fleshy constructs & this room
is constructed of hopeful encounters & enthusiasm
for *Cardcaptors* but ur more in2
Sailor Moon. & ur in2 me
apparently.
coz u ask if i wanna surf
down ur information superhighway.
even tho i'm states away & don't live
near a beach. even tho i don't know
who the Sailor Starlights r but i research them

with increased interest &
repulsion. finally i answer, witty & confused:
21/dunno/my house
JussSumGuy: o_0
JussSumGuy: U DUNNO WTF??
Luv2SK8: i think i'm in between y'know?
JussSumGuy: UR SICK N GROSS
JussSumGuy has left the room
Luv2SK8:

```
......................./˝~/)
...................,/˜../
.................../..../
............./˝~/'..'/'˜˜`;
........../"/.../.../..../˜¨\
........("(...´...´.... ˜~/>...»)
.........\..................',...../
.........."...\..........._.'
...........\..............(
.............\..............\...
```

who, what, why, where
(A Google predictive search poem)

who do I look like?   what are your strengths?
who are you?   what is happening?
who are traditional owners?   what is the time?
who are the kardashians?   what is tripe?
who are the transgenders?   what is transgender?

why is the sky blue?   where am I?
why am I so tired?   where are the fireworks tonight?
why are you running?   where are you now?
why are they called march flies?   where are the snowflakes?
why are trees green?   where are the tonsils?
why are trans fats unhealthy?   where are the training dummies?
why are transformers needed?   where are the transition metals?
why are transgenders?   where are the transgenders?

assumptions not classified

this ambiguous reading " this their is nor them or any that ,
defying what is dismantled and denied

artist scratches of . of painter's and captures of . of the world
appropriated exercise or abstraction of this blame-like brush

supposed . to have those limitations however binary
but ,,

art declines rules on painted binary paintings
ways of beings are paintings

'imagine thinking conventionally like cisgender'
binary behest forgone because ..

radical bodies represent : with metaphor
peeling this predetermined , this absent trope

physical , . art . is defiantly colour

Request /	/ Response
As per transhuman protocol I respond only in digits. But number me up like butter and I'll tell you "everything"	

		About gender?	300 Multiple Choices
		My gender?	423 Locked
A selfie?	A screenshot?	A nude?	402 Payment Required
		That question?	425 Too Early We just
		fucking	met
		Can you curb	your curiosity?
		Oh	417 Expectation Failed ...

	My ""surgeries""?	400 Bad Request
My tackle	My downstairs	429 Too Many Requests
My between-legs	My ""sex"?"?	403 Forbidden

Your hand,	just there?	406 Not Acceptable
Your insistence your persistence your languid excuses?		409 Conflict

Your hand,	again?	401 Unauthorised
	My slap?	102 Processing
	Cheek ricochet?	201 Created
	Your inquest?	410 Gone

My dignity?	302 Found

Rainbow confetti pixels

Coming out as non-binary is like yelling into a void but
the void has disappeared and been replaced by change
rooms in Target and they're not even echoey enough
to surround-sound your voice so you can yell, 'Oi! I'm
neither of these, mate!' Instead, they're just small stalls
getting smaller and smaller and playing the same 80s and
90s hits on repeat. Every damn time. You're ushered and
tense. Rinse repeat. You could rebel

but you don't. You enter the change room but it's actually a
toilet cubicle … coz at the end of the day being trans is all
about fucking loos, am I right? Coming out as non-binary
is you staring big-eyed at the toilet who's flapping their
lid saying, 'Feed me!' kinda like in that 80s show *The Trap
Door* … coz all trans kids grew up in the late 80s/early 90s
and never aged and none of them can be older or younger
than me … coz it's all just a fad like butterfly clips and
Tamagotchis, am I right?

But they're back. Tamagotchis. You can feed them and
clean their poop just like you could back in the day …
coz back in my day I was still searching the mobile library
shelves for books and words that described who I was.
Coz coming out as non-binary is a whole goddamn
lifelong process

like: Step 1. Brush the poop of your binary existence out
the door with a pixelated broom. Step 2. Replace the
poop with butterfly clips in all different colours, mirroring

your bedroom's purposefully rainbowed bookshelf. Step 3. Scatter 100s and 1000s like rainbow confetti pixels in the air. Step 4. Yell, 'Just fuck off, mate!' to the demanding toilet binarists and their ""transtrender"" theories … coz today's trans trend is not feeding the trap door. All those monsters. Today's trans trend is feeding yourself love and goodness. Today's trans trend is believing

you are non-binary enough, no matter what the monsters say.

Today's trans truth is that we've always been here. 100s and 1000s of years of us existing and echoing in surround-sound pixel-filled skies, writing our words and stories into the historic void, coming out on repeat. Rinse repeat. Rebel repeat. Every damn time. But never … ever … disappearing …

Exhale

levitate me, lover
For Ray

it takes two trans people   to sext   without naming
to touch   every inch   without measuring
to say *wet* and *slick*   without saying   *how*
to say *come* and *for me*   without saying   *with what*

to say spoon me   our bodies fit   perfectly because
the purpose   of your spine   is for curving yourself
against me

to say push   your fingerprints   against my hand
like palmistry   please   clasp my knuckles
like we're praying   because goddamn   if this
isn't holy

to say fill me up   fill the space beside me on top beneath me
with your softness   your warm dewy   lawn-scented skin
I want to fill you   put my fingers   in your mouth
spit-soaked   writhing   look into your eyes
while I fuck you

fuck you   body against hungry   body because
we're all just skin   against sea salt sweat   against itching skin
against the world
just typing   texting   touching   and conjuring revolution
in our beds

bodies / your body

wrap my arms around
your body / fingers interlinking / never stretching
far enough to envelop
the circumference of you.
trickle my fingernails across
each tattoo / along blank slate
skin / soft hair thickets / shave
day prickles. reach to caress etched jaw / rounded
pimpled   sagging cheek / mouth ajar
closed   open   eyelids   wide-eyed
glittering   eyelashes   quivering.

your body.
your body is good to me.
hand small enough to fan-fold and push
inside me / big enough to grip my whole
neck like you could crush me
but don't. I'm in love with your
ampleness / your flatness / your stone
muscled fitness / your spilling stomach
over your skirt.

your body.
I'm bisexual for your body
coz your skin tastes
of seasons / your brown sunscreen
sea salt skin / your bitter to tongue-lick
perfumed skin / your sweet-scented cloud-plumped skin.
your butter thighs / glassware-smooth / weighted

with stretch mark rivulets / meandering wrinkles / scars
blemishes   husked   indents   stretched
flesh for clutching   grasping   bruising
with my hands as I kiss
your purple lipsticked lips / your chapped
quivering moaning lips / your full
areola-tinged lips.
good god your body
your bodies are good.

to voyage with loved ones who transition

{1}

it's an honour to be with you here at brink
& beginning. a joy to listen as new words breach
your lips & shape space in our mouths
& this room. a privilege to touch
your changing body, my fingers drifting
against the hem of new skirt, palm resting
against neck's first choker. i'm no saint. i refuse ovation
or flattery that this must be 'so hard'.   it's not.
you have never not been Her & i am humbled
to be with you here
& here
& here

{2}

i couldn't do what you do, he said,
couldn't love, like … that …

but what if (& hear me out)
you did?

{3}

when daylight fails
to warm heart-
space and stamina
remember this: I see you
I see you and you
are nothing short of
glorious

Periphery

1.

I am goose flesh
and sticky. You are orbiting,
tight-muscled and
concentrating roughly
on the shape of me,
on the space between
where our eyes meet
and the tiling starts. Far
periphery: the boundary
you haven't yet crossed, radius
where flesh meets
uncharted. You unzip
me and I almost
unnerve. Layers
fan and unfurl like sliced
bread. Your pupils jitter
like houseflies as you back
off, spooked.

Later, alone,
I slice tomato for sandwiches, bread
knife dividing bright swollen
flesh, withdrawing wet and seed-soaked.

2.

I am orbiting, observing
as you sit, sticky and
swollen on the kitchen
bench. I close the space
between us, nudging against
the shape of you. Your pupils
dilate, eyelids flicker
closed, as I lick the radius
of your neck, from collar
bone to ear. You unzip
me, I unfurl. A housefly
jitters past as you sink
forward, euphoric.

Later, you hold me,
tight-muscled, sweat-
soaked, as we lay fanned
and goose fleshed
on the tiles.

this one room
With thanks to Rico Craig

let's play house! let's mop coffee marks
from studio's length. chew less gum
& give our teeth a real good scrub.
we can move against or with
Time. whatever we want. we can do
whatever we want!

+

let's play house! let's call Love
slowly to supper. cook Her meals
like we're a fancy-ass restaurant
with some smooth background
bryan ferry. yet all we have left
is a woolies rationed basics box
& a tiny-ass camp stove &
construction whines from next door.

+

let's play house! Time can stop
by but Stress won't leave,
burrows keenly like Cat
digging up our roses. i miss her
rosy nose. i miss privilege of pace
like trailing ants, exploring …

clean 'em up with paper towels
throw 'em in laundry basket,
rich smell of their bodies
crushed like garbage.

+

let's play house! window glare streaks
lightning across bed sheets.
leg hair glimmers with fairy light
sirens. you softly hum-snore
as autumn turns winter. all in
this one room.

=

Cat down the street is faster
than Time. zigzag bolts
from us. procures a new family
new home new suburb. all while
we're syrupy like old
sticky notes. i miss her
& i miss you. even when
you're in this room.

please come back. come over.
let's play house xx

we've got this

step 5. skip to the middle. you've been
disassociating. fragments of steps 1, 2, 3 and 4:
dry hands, glass jars of pasta, blood flecks on fabric
when you jab your finger sewing face masks.
step 6. hold her closer as evenings
creep colder. tell her you'll be okay.
step 10. skip ahead. spoiler alert: we'll be okay.
step 7, 8. 'I've got this,' you say, hoisting jar
from top shelf. step 9. boil pasta in low evening light
as she tans the onions. fold your arms around her.

What if we
After Tyza Hart's exhibition 'To and From the River' (STABLE, 2019)

Four strangers enter riverspace.
      Four flat-lie on pontoon: spines
            stretched prone on timber. River
      beneath splashing sparklers
in the sky. Like at 16 when I calligraphed
      my crush's name with fireworks
            against fading night. And now
      when my skin fizzes like 20-cent sherbet
at the warmth of three bodies

            so close to mine.
                Stars backdrop
                    pulses of water
                and rippled words
            surface above us.
                My lips gasp
                    dryly, my heart
                pitches open.
            What if, scribes the river,
                            you all
                                just kissed?

gilled and :: glow ...

please hold on : tight-en : the grip of your hand on my :
hip : flattens and goose pimples at your vapour : touch : me
like you love all the gasping flaws of : me : and you are the
same twin glow of : pine : tree at my etch-worn back as
you flush red in the cold : air : flutters in butterfly draughts
past your blush-gilled cheeks and I'm under I'm under :::...

XX
For Cassie

a bolder me would have asked to kiss
        you that day: the prayerful fluke
        of finding ourselves alone and queer

in that dressing room. your summer skin
        feverish against my own. my open
        palm against your shoulder blades

as offering.

Safe words

I know one thing:
I want the jawbreaker
glass of your collarbone
in my mouth. Memories of
crooked finger, strangle-
hooked to the underside
of your chin: lifting gills
wider, neck taller (all the better
to bite down on, dearest).
My other hand? Forever fixed
to your shoulder, pinning you
like butterfly but wingless but
soaring because I still know
one thing: this high
is the safest
we've ever been.

when I said I wanted to be choked
this is not what I meant

night before it all
went up – flung mask
from tabletop, shoved it
to your lips. other hand at
neck: our soft heartbeats
in my palm. *okay?* I say.
more, you mumble.

next day – the best
of our possessions
in the back seat.
my palm tensed
on your thigh as you
drive: radio grating, windows
down, face masks fixed.
okay? you mumble. *no
more*, I say.

aglow, I inhale

awash on the rubble sand
we embrace. you chitter me love
notes, chirping lips tickling my sternum, pinching
my sticky skin between your teeth. you tug
with a growl, black eyes impish.

my love, undress me.

a sharp slice like tearing
fabric rings round our cave
walls. the glint of my scream
summons shadows.

your mouth swollen
with blood as you squat
astride my hips, gleeful
mouthful. my pulsing heart
where your tongue should be.
       you wink   eyelashes fanning.
       teeth aglow   you bite down.

I arch and swell, exhaling in gushes, ribs creaking
like ship's hull. your birdsong ripples
in my ears.

I inhale.

Dirty, clean

*Write me like one of your good
girls*, they gasp, lips slack and dirty
with language, body splayed
like tapestry. Glossed light
singes weave curtains, while we warp
and weft, tracing wordless skin, nails
and knife grazing sharp calligraphy.

I fill them up with words
to tip them out. They pour
all over my thighs. Drizzled

threads coat their tummy, skin flushed
red with ruckus. Their gushed
endearments wash me
clean.

seaworthy~

our genitals siren-call to ships ~ startle
men with searchlight shafts ~ mock and moor them
off the coast ~ hulls hitched in fine-spun sand
like their heads: cu(n)t~splice~clamped
betwixt thighs ~ I could roil and twist your
skull clean ~ capsize and careen you
      baptismal ~ leave you buoyant~ port side~
      anew

likeness of submersions

```
(ocean mist)   moist      shower        water          steaming
pink (sea      foam)      tinted        shampoo        suds
slim           crimson    (precious     coral) eager   mouth
damp           tile-      flattened     (sea           grass) spine
roaming        water-     wrinkled      fingertips     (anemone)

                          {encroaching  {blooming}     anemone
{venom         {branching                flowering}    anemone
                          slits of      {flesh}        anemone
frenzy                    peak          spasm}         anemone
```

Exalt

you hold a lot of tension in your   body

take *girl* & the hesitant   choked   *sorry*
so sorry & slot it   brittle   & spiky
with others   of its kind: under purple
polished nail of   right   index finger.

will that be all   *today*   *ma'am?*
clasp the word with   my receipt   fold it
paper-fanned   against my   spine.

my shoulder   has hurt   for weeks.
the physio punctures   skin, dry   needle
tapping echoes   against bone.
how does that feel?   as he withdraws, a trickle
of airline announcements   *ladies*   *& gentlemen*
tumbles out.   *better,*   I say.
like ghosts,   I think.   we ice it
& I feel *she's* and *hers*   gathering   against shoulder
blades. *it might hurt*   *for a day*   *or two.*

at the party. mulled   red wine dulls
pain & cackle laughter   & fire pit crackling
lights up   familiar faces.
my frame loosens.   my defences draw
back like an   awning. walking home
I hold twinkles of   *theys* & *thems*
& true-names in my   coat pockets.
they candle-flicker   through fabric.

alone, under our house,
one by one, roll
from palm to palm, drop
into hammock, flanked
of our house. I ease
rock and rollick
of respectful voices:
rae they rae

I pluck them
them admiringly
each one
to the limbs
myself into them
among the hum
they rae they
they rae

flourish, viola
For the Viola banksii

flourish   a shady
moist area

            botanical
                        seed
dispersal

                                    the
capsule open
        & seed pod splits
boat-shaped   each
                        dark seed
packed neatly and tightly

                                dries
and shrinks
            narrows and squeezes
                        wet marble between
your fingers
            wonder   in

bright purple

the good boy
For Jesse, Charlie and Zoë

the boy languishes, takes stock
of sunbeams, pivots angular
into yogic side twist, twirls again
to dart in spurts, burbling each
burst, before energy evaporates
and he curls c-shaped to lick
his undercarriage

two figures

```
                              s
            i  l              h
          t        e          a
        c             &       d
       a              s       o
       t             m        w
                     o        e
                     o        d
                     t
                     h
```

The three genders: women, men, consumerism

Gifts for her: delicate pretty
dainty charming girly
female jewellery
up to 50% off!!! Our new
black sleek electric
razor, only $299
will make you instantly
manlier and somehow
more ripped! confident!
heroic! virile! Versatile: use it to subdue
your pubes or mince all those
carrots (only two bucks a kilo!)
But she uses it to shave her legs
then deliberately combs up
her foot, severing
the ornamental anklet.
Tiny silver links catch
against titanium like gravel-jangle
in Sunday's motor mower. Later
he uses the razor to prune his
underarms, the anklet's trinkets
replace his pit hair and he looks
like Christmas: globes suspended
weighty and glinting. Winking
she says, *you look good*. Dazzled
he says, *I feel golden*.

destination. journey :

he.or.she he.or.she
his.or.hers his.or.hers
the 3 genders
& I'm the 'or'.
| : |
he.or.she his.or.hers
what does it take
to lengthen a train
to add more carriages
to jump aboard?
| : |
his.or.hers theirs.or.vers
zirs.or.hirs pers.or.oursss
ssscraped by commotion
the rails screeeeech.
| : |
we're here. come
aboard. let's stow
our baggage, sit right
up the back.
| : |
his.or.hers.or.theirs.or
now, let me tell you
how to lean gently on
one another without
rocking sideways.

Worlds, woven

For Ray

Long distance: an almost non-issue when blessed with inter-
locking layers. Veils flicker and collide between your world
and mine. We're shopping on the same Tuesday
and I gasp to see you glitch forward in front of me:
flecks of you picking boxes, browsing.
>   *Reckon we should get some tea?*

And the cat: the same black-tailed girl
we pat in different states. Our witchy courier
of love notes. I crouch to greet her, feel sun-glazed
fur on my palm, feel the purr of your breath
on my cheek.
>   *Guess what? I love you.*
>   *So much.*

And then there are walls
near our beds, opposite sides.
Sometimes clasping coldness through
sleepiness means I can taste the warmth
of your hand rippling through brick.
>   *Hold me, babe. Wake me tomorrow*
>   *to spoon me. Shift back the weave curtains*
>   *to let light in, so we can always love*
>   *like this.*

clear skies
For Mark

seashells picked & palmed, swelling
lips sun-kissed like glinting
waves. i cup conch between
fingers & drink
you in. today
      we are sunbeams.

Abundantly blue
After FLOURISH, Leanne Vincent, 2020

Deliberate heel-toe on time-worn soil, lap
upon lap upon dizzying blue lap
around blueprint backyard. I breathe
blue air to ease confinement, blue breath
skimming and swallowing the sky.
On blue-lined paper with blue-ink pen
I note: each blue petal of blue agapanthus,
bold blue bug on blue-sizzling rock.
With each tiny, tightened observation
I feel slower, calmer, bluely decadent.
There's abundance here. A treetop rustles
as a blue-faced honeyeater takes flight.

Wheelie bin
For Kate Durbin

Day softly overcast. Breeze
pushing back 8am humidity.
Lined up on next door's rooftop:
8 honeyeaters, 1 kookaburra.
Easing the day forward with
       squabbles, preening &
       morning-soft banter.

At 12pm, clouds shiver
& threaten clean laundry.
The rush to close
open windows when we hear
the thunder-like rumble
       of a wheelie bin
       returning home.

queer platonic love

let us be
the kind of friends
who hold hands, who
when pressed
palm-to-palm say
yes,
we are a couple
of queers who spoon
each other to sleep:
2 ginger cats
warmly curled
under blankets when the cold
snap hits. who kiss
tops of shaved heads,
stroke long hair
on legs and new spikes
on chins. who fall asleep
on the bus, stacked
shoulder-&-heads
and I relish the wheat-
skin scent of you. let us be

the kind of friends
who hold hands: loosely,
tightly, sun-up-to-midnight,
over decades:
from days   of warm   elastic skin
to seasons   of paperbark   stretched
            over knuckles   swelling.

dearest friend,

our hands meet
tectonic. edges soften as thumb
scores palm. half-moon loops
tracing your heart line. tonight
you are loved. tonight we are
boundless.

it's all just meta, baby

polyamory
can be confusing   until you think of it   like a steaming Hot
Mess during summer when everyone   agrees it's a brilliant day for a
BBQ but you end up giving   up & ordering three large pizzas
& free garlic bread because   it's summer   in Queensland
& we might be kinky but we're not   fucking masochists
who thirst for a day spent   feeling dizzy, faces dripping
over sizzling vego sausages

so   if you think of polyamory
as this collaborative enthusiasm   to eat carbs & nap
underneath the only overhead fan   in the house   like a house
party that's always happening   but it's in separate locations like your
house, my flat,   their hotel, on Twitter   & everyone's talking
& interacting   & loving   & feeling   & queerfully

gleaming with the community of it all   then maybe   it's not the weirdest
thing you've ever heard of

in fact   maybe it's the most lovely   & comforting   of all things
maybe it's the calmest & happiest   i've ever been   coz non-monogamy
is pretty rad   but also sometimes   pretty randy   let's be honest:
like when you masturbated   thinking about hir masturbating
thinking about him masturbating   thinking about me & like when i see you
kiss eir cheek   & nuzzle eir neck   & it's all i can do not to cry
big goddamn tears of   happiness   in the knowledge
that this is the glorious life   we have woven   with each other

house hunters

the land next door
is up for sale.
masked lapwings
on high-rise limbs
prowl construction site
ground: 'if it flat, we nest.'
bright white Queenslander
propped high
on Jenga blocks
awaits next month's
big move: five inches
forward, one inch right.
men till the ground
mow
clip
cut
fell.
it all grows back
within a week
and is left to the house
hunting lapwings
and their pink galah
kin: squawking
and rummaging
the overgrown earth,
always after
the latest seeds,
always
after

what's
next.

not unlike love

it's something to do with impermanence.
the flight-swift slice of limb
from log, bone from branch.
about the smallest snips it took
to ground you.

it's something not unlike possession.
about fell from falling, freedom from
freefall. the quick cleave of chainsaws
then corellas screeching
treeless.

if eviction's in moratorium, then does private
equal public? and what might it mean to grow
autonomy? in the hot bask of afternoon sun
I kneel to count your notches and tally
your timeline and you tell me
we could be happy here.

and so we dig and turn, plant
parsley and basil, chives and mint.
we laugh at aphids, leafhoppers,
landlords and other pests.
we knock down the gates

and the for sale sign.
we let the sun in.

trans   (gender)

1) bodies with limitless   narratives
2) absence of binaries
3) inclusive of exploration
4) skin anointed in tribute

a) affirming portraiture
b) no reductive bullshit
c) fluidity like blended paint
d) we traverse

transcend

I am myself

exactly as I am   I am myself as self   but myself in motion

as moon-infused quartz   and multi-verse   not just the in-between

but the fluidity   the change   and the motion   of motion

of my prophecy   never forecast   or fulfilled

not just non-binary   but ongoing   and changing   nourishing the constant motion

the change   the pleasure   of indecisiveness   of broken

winter clock   who's always in time   and never on time

time as construct   colonial gender   as construct and constant

take clock apart   in the sunshine   reflective and reflection

my fluid reflection   in your honest   queer words

not just queer   but queer   as in joyful

not just the present   but the future   and the future's future

not just me   but also you   and you and you

and you and you and you and you and you and you and you and you and you and you and you a
nd you and you and you and you and you and you and you and you and you and you and you and
you and you and you and you and you and you and you and you and you and you and you and yo

u and you and you and you and you and you and you an
d you and you and you and you and you and you
and you and you and you and you and yo
u and you and you and you and y
ou and you and you and y
ou and you and yo
u and you
and y
o
n

Notes

Many poems in this collection use gender-neutral pronouns, that is, pronouns that aren't he/him/his or she/her/hers. Examples include: they/them/theirs, ve/ver/vers, zie/zim/zirs, ze/hir/hirs, ey/em/eirs and per/per/pers.

'Do more, do better' was commissioned for *Cordite 87: DIFFICULT.* Accompanying art pieces and a critical statement (*The Unaugmented Reality of Transgender Discrimination: 'Do more, do better'*) are available at cordite. org.au. Big queer thanks to Emory Black, who was my artistic partner in this venture, and to Kent MacCarter and Rosalind McFarlane at *Cordite* for commissioning the work.

': paint me over', 'assumptions not classified', 'two figures' and 'trans (gender)' are ekphrastic poems commissioned for the exhibition *Assuming a Surface* by Tyza Hart and James Barth at the Walls Gallery in Miami, Gold Coast. For 'assumptions not classified' I took Caity Reynolds's essay on *Assuming a Surface* and used the text manipulator glass. leaves (glassleaves.herokuapp.com) to scramble all the words. This is but a portion of the randomised, hauntingly accurate result. Reproduced by kind permission of Caity Reynolds.

'if there's nothing out there, why am I searching?' – aerial roots on succulent plants sometimes form when a plant isn't getting enough water. They use these roots to search for moisture in humid air.

'home watchful and dust' was created using Zalgo Text (lingojam.com/ZalgoText generator), which is creepy glitch text made up of many Unicode diacritic marks.

'Gender marker' and 'wanna cyber??? ;)))' contain ASCII art: pictures made from the characters defined by ASCII compliant character sets.

'Discussing polyamory in the workplace:' is inspired by and with respect to Zenobia Frost's poem 'Census Night' (*After the Demolition*, Cordite Books, 2019).

'the island rule(r)' – the fossilised remains of the world's largest-known rabbit, *Nuralagus rex*, were found on the small Mediterranean island of Minorca in 2011. The 'Minorcan King of the Rabbits' was six times the size of most rabbits today and lived three to five million years ago. As per 'the island rule', small animals often grow larger when living on isolated islands without predators. Ōkunoshima is a small island in the Inland Sea of Japan – presently, hundreds of feral rabbits call this island home.

'I've got something to say' is a response poem to Alex the Astronaut's song 'Not Worth Hiding'.

'this one room' was commissioned for the Red Dirt Poetry Festival 2020, as part of an online collaborative work Poetry First Aid House. The piece uses poetry techniques taught in Rico Craig's Queensland Poetry Festival workshop 'The Everyday Epic'.

'seaworthy~' – cut/cunt splice is a join between two lines, where each rope end is fixed to the other a short distance along to make an opening that closes under tension.

'flourish, viola' was originally a blackout poem using text from the Society for Growing Australian Plants bulletin, June 2014. Reproduced by kind permission of Native Plants Queensland.

Acknowledgements

This book was written on the unceded lands of the Jagera and Turrbal people. I pay my deepest respects to Elders past and present. Always was, always will be.

Thank you to *Aniko Press*, *Aoetearotica*, *Antithesis Journal*, *Australian Poetry Journal* and *Anthology*, *Baby Teeth Journal*, *Blue Bottle Journal*, *Concrescence*, *Cordite Poetry Review*, *foam:e*, *Groundswell: The Overland Judith Wright Poetry Prize for New and Emerging Poets 2007–2020*, *Hecate*, *honey & lime lit*, *Island Magazine*, *Melbourne Spoken Word*, *Perverse*, *post ghost press*, *Rabbit*, Red Dirt Poetry Festival, *Stilts Journal*, *Subbed In: Ibis House*, *The Tundish Review*, *Twisted Moon Magazine*, *Umbel & Panicle*, *Vulture Bones* and *Westerly* for previously publishing poems from this book.

Thank you to judges Judith Beveridge and Kirli Saunders for awarding 'The last tourist' Highest Queensland Entry in the 2020 Val Vallis Award; to judge Pip Smith for shortlisting 'who, what, why, where' (in its visual art iteration on *Baby Teeth Journal*) in the 2020 Woollahra Digital Literary Awards; and to judges Annie Solah and Melanie Mununggurr for awarding 'Hussshhh' Highest Queensland Entry in the 2019 XYZ Prize for Innovation in Spoken Word.

Immense gratitude to my editor Felicity Plunkett for her encouragement, enthusiasm and expertise. And to the wonderful team at UQP, including my publisher Aviva Tuffield, project editor Cathy Vallance and publicist Jean

Smith: thank you for your warmth and dedication to this book.

Much love to my key friendship groups: the ever-talented Poet Pals, and the always-brilliant Trivia Kings, Queens & iNBetweens. Big hugs to Jesse, Charlie and Zoë; and to Robyn, Grace, Alison and Tegan. Love to my loves: Cam, Cassie, Charity, Chris, Kieran, Mark and Ray/Rei. And to my parents: your support of my work has been generous and immeasurable, thank you. I have so much love to give and I love every single one of you so very much.